COLONIAL PEOPLE

The Surveyor

CHRISTINE PETERSEN

Marshall Cavendish
Benchmark
New York

Website: www.marshallcavendish.us

This publication represents the opinions and views of the author based on Christine Petersen's personal experience, knowledge,
and research. The information in this book serves as a general guide only. The author and publisher have used their best efforts
in preparing this book and disclaim liability rising directly and indirectly from the use and application of this book.

Other Marshall Cavendish Offices:

Marshall Cavendish International (Asia) Private Limited, 1 New Industrial Road, Singapore 536196 • Marshall Cavendish
International (Thailand) Co Ltd. 253 Asoke, 12th Flr, Sukhumvit 21 Road, Klongtoey Nua, Wattana, Bangkok 10110,
Thailand • Marshall Cavendish (Malaysia) Sdn Bhd, Times Subang, Lot 46, Subang Hi-Tech Industrial Park, Batu Tiga,
40000 Shah Alam, Selangor Darul Ehsan, Malaysia

Marshall Cavendish is a trademark of Times Publishing Limited

All websites were available and accurate when this book was sent to press.

Library of Congress Cataloging-in-Publication Data

Petersen, Christine.
The surveyor / by Christine Petersen.
p. cm. — (Colonial people)
Summary: "Explores the life of a colonial surveyor and his importance to the community, as well as everyday life,
responsibilities, and social practices during that time"—Provided by publisher.
Includes bibliographical references and index.
ISBN 978-0-7614-4805-1
Surveying—United States—History—18th century—Juvenile literature.
Surveyors—United States—History—18th century—Juvenile literature.
Title.
TA521.P48 2011
526.90973'09033—dc22
2009033497

Editor: Christine Florie
Publisher: Michelle Bisson
Art Director: Anahid Hamparian
Series Designer: Kay Petronio

Expert Reader: Paul Douglas Newman, Ph.D., Department of History, University of Pittsburgh at Johnstown

Photo research by Marybeth Kavanagh

Cover photo by The Granger Collection, New York

The photographs in this book are used by permission and through the courtesy of:
The Granger Collection, New York: 4, 11, 12, 26, 38, 39; *Getty Images*: MPI, 8; *The Colonial Williamsburg Foundation*:
16, 18, 23, 32, 36; *Everett Collection*: 17; *Corbis*: Bettmann, 31; *North Wind Picture Archives*: 41

Printed in Malaysia (T)
1 3 5 6 4 2

CONTENTS

ONE

Settling the New World

North America must have looked like paradise to English explorers who visited in 1584. Their ships sailed into shallow waters that were clear and clean. The men hunted and fished until their bellies and storage boxes were full. Along the shorelines they found wild grapes growing thickly among the trees. One sailor wrote home of the sight, exclaiming, "I think in all the world the like abundance is not to be found." Equally impressive was the variety of foods grown by local American Indians, who kept farms all along the Atlantic coastline. Eager to settle in this fine New World, the sailors claimed the land on behalf of England.

English colonists arrived a year later. They chose a small island just south of Chesapeake Bay, in what is now Virginia, as the site of their settlement. The local Algonquin Indians called

English colonists land on Roanoke Island and establish the first colony in America.

this island Roanoke, and the name stuck. A small, tidy settlement was established, with houses and a fort. Settlers explored inland and along the coast, creating detailed drawings and maps of this remarkable region.

But Roanoke was not destined to become the first permanent English colony in America. The colonists did not get along well with local American Indians. And they were completely unprepared for the demands of farming. By the end of winter, their food supplies began to run low. When a fleet of English warships passed by in June 1586, most of the colonists returned to England on the ships.

Trying Again

Failure at Roanoke did not dash the hope for an English colony in the New World. Two groups of citizens became especially interested in obtaining land there. Businessmen believed that the New World was a land of riches. They planned to harvest wood, metals, and other valuable natural resources to sell in England. Religious groups such as the Puritans and Quakers sought a place to worship freely, away from the strict rules of the Church of England. In 1606 King James I of England granted permission for colonization to begin anew. Colonists were free to pursue their dreams.

As at Roanoke, a life of hardships awaited the small group of colonists. Days were spent in a struggle to clear land for crops, houses, and villages. In the winter of 1607, half of the colonial population died of colds, influenza, and other diseases. Warm weather brought a different collection of ordeals: clouds of mosquitoes, long days of backbreaking work, and deep loneliness. Men often came without their families. Colonial families left behind relatives, belongings, and everything familiar from their past lives.

Despite these challenges, most colonists stuck it out in their new home. They were joined by increasing numbers of immigrants each year. In 1630 about 4,600 colonists could be found in two colonial settlements at Jamestown, Virginia, and Plymouth, Massachusetts. The population grew to 50,000 in twenty years. As the colonial era came to a close in 1770, the number of white settlers in England's thirteen North American colonies was close to 2 million.

A Man of Many Skills

People had many reasons for coming to the colonies. The earliest colonists at Jamestown thought only of finding gold and other precious minerals. These men intended to return to England as soon as they struck it rich. Within a few decades the colonists'

By the mid–1600s, Jamestown, Virginia, was a growing settlement and became the capital of the Virginia Colony.

Selling the Settlers

In its early years Jamestown Colony was in constant need of money. To attract more investors and paying settlers, clever English businessmen prepared flyers describing the beauty and natural wealth of the New World.

The land yieldeth naturally for the sustenance of man, abundance of fish, both scale and shell; of land and water fowls, infinite store; of deer . . . and hares, with many fruits and roots.

There are valleys and plains streaming with sweet springs, like veins in a natural body; there are hills and mountains making a sensible proffer of hidden treasure, never yet searched. The land is full of minerals, plenty of woods [the wants of England] . . . the soil is strong and lusty of its own nature.

The advertising worked. English colonists came in hopes of collecting their share of New World treasure. They paid the fare and made the long ocean journey. It soon became clear that everything in the flyers had been a lie. Parts of North America might be lush and abundant, but Jamestown had been built in the middle of a swamp. The colonists would be lucky to survive, let alone find treasure.

view began to change. Many saw America as a new home, and they shared two dreams: the opportunity to exercise personal freedom and to own land. In England, land ownership had been limited to the wealthy and powerful. Every free male colonist had the right to own property. Land quickly became the measure of a colonist's wealth. It gave him control and a voice in his community.

Distribution of land depended on the surveyor, the expert who measured and mapped the land. As a result, he became one of the most influential men in colonial society. His profession required skill in math and science, writing, and art. Yet the surveyor was also a hardy outdoorsman who could stand the most difficult conditions. He spent weeks or months away from home, traveling through unexplored countryside to discover which lands would be suitable for settlement.

The surveyor's job was not only to explore the land. He was expected to describe and map it in great detail. Surveying involved measurement at many scales—from the borders of entire colonies to the boundaries of tiny farms. The surveyor walked up hills to determine their **elevation** and braved rivers to find their depth. Governments also relied on the surveyor to design colonial towns, cities, and systems of roads. The growth of America's young colonies was measured by his work.

The colonial surveyor was comfortable in the great outdoors and spent days at a time surveying the open lands of America.

Dividing up the Land

Colonial governments were allowed to distribute land by any system they chose. Landowner William Penn leased sections of his massive property, called Pennsylvania, to Quakers and other colonists. The colony of Maryland took a similar approach.

Its government offered small farms to fit the budgets of its poor Catholic and Protestant settlers. Puritan colonists in New England bought land as a community.

In Virginia land was handed out in two ways. **Shareholders** automatically received 1,000 **acres** each upon arriving in the colony. These colonists had given money to support expeditions from England. Other Virginia settlers received land in a system called **headright**. The idea was simple. Each man who paid a large passage fare to come to Virginia received 50 acres of land in

Parceled and fenced-off land is plowed by a farmer in colonial North Carolina.

exchange for that fare (one acre is equal to 43,560 square feet). If he had also paid to bring over family members or servants, the man received an additional 50 acres per person.

Poor Englishmen had no way to pay for their journey across the ocean. These people often signed contracts to become indentured servants. Under the system of **indenture**, a wealthy colonist paid to bring workers to the colonies. He provided food and a place for the workers to live. Englishmen who could afford to bring many indentured servants to the colonies had the potential to collect large blocks of land.

Some Had No Freedom

It was not long before large property owners found that they needed more help than indentured servants could provide. American Indians were the first slaves on colonial farms. Beginning in the 1660s, millions of African people were taken from their homes and sold to colonial landowners. Slavery became commonplace even in the cities. In 1687 one traveler noted that "there is not a house in Boston, however small may be its name, that has not one or two." Very few of these slaves could hope to become free, let alone to own land.

TWO

Studying to Survey

As each colonial boy reached the age of thirteen or so, a serious question arose in his family. What would be his profession? Most boys had no choice in this matter. A father considered his son's skills and looked around for options in the community. Many jobs were learned through hands-on experience and training. For example, a blacksmith could not learn his trade from books. He had to work in a smithy, becoming familiar with the tools of his trade.

A boy might learn surveying in several ways. Numerous colonial schools and colleges offered programs in this profession. Students at the College of Philadelphia learned complex mathematics, navigation, and astronomy. Pennsylvania's Kent County School suggested that a successful surveyor should also study English, Latin, writing, and bookkeeping.

Families that could not afford this option might purchase a

book on surveying. Many classic surveying texts were published in England throughout the colonial era. But English surveying books were not ideal for use in America. England was a land of gently rolling hills, farmland, pastures, and small patches of forest. This open landscape made the surveyor's job simpler. He could easily move from place to place and had a good view across the landscape. The colonial surveyor's job was entirely different. He had to hack through thick forests and often could not see more than a few trees ahead. In 1688 a famous English surveyor named John Love wrote a book specifically about surveying in America. He called it *Geodaesia: or, The Art of Surveying and Measuring of Land Made Easy*. Love's book described the use of surveying instruments that were appropriate for America's challenging terrain. *Geodaesia* also covered essential mathematics and mapping skills. A hardworking boy could study the book and learn much about surveying on his own.

The most common way to become a surveyor was through an apprenticeship. In this system, the boy learned by working with an experienced surveyor. Surveying apprenticeships might last a few months or as much as seven years. Whatever the length of time, the relationship was considered an indenture. It was made legal through a contract. The **apprentice** promised to serve his master, doing whatever work was asked of him. In return, the master agreed to provide a home and food for the apprentice. He promised to teach the boy all the skills needed to become a successful surveyor and to provide him with the tools of the trade when his apprenticeship was complete.

A young apprentice learns surveying skills from his master.

The Most Famous Surveyor

In 1744 thirteen-year-old George Washington sat in his classroom at the Henry Williams School in colonial Virginia. He didn't care much for reading but found math fascinating. When his teacher began lessons on surveying, George took notice. This subject combined math and his other favorite pastime: being outside. He made notes in a schoolbook describing the job:

Surveying is the Art of Measuring Land and it consists of 3 parts.
1st The going round and measuring a piece of Wood Land
2nd Plotting the same and 3rd to find the content thereof.

Three years later George found his father's old surveying tools. He practiced by surveying his older brother's turnip patch. Soon George was invited to help on a real survey in the rich farming land of Virginia's Shenandoah Valley. The survey team faced nasty weather, wild animals, and even a fire in George's tent. George loved the work anyway and decided to become a professional surveyor, but he only got to do it for a few years. In 1754 George Washington was called up to join the army. The young surveyor would later become a great general—and the first president of the United States of America.

Lines and Directions

The apprentice might begin learning the trade by reading about surveying instruments. There were many pieces of equipment that could make a land survey more accurate. Two were absolutely essential: a set of measuring chains and a **compass**. Colonial surveyors measured distances using long chains made from iron links. These are called Gunter's chains, named after their inventor.

The colonial surveyor relied on his compass to maintain the direction for a straight property boundary line.

Gunter's chains were usually made in 66-foot lengths containing a hundred links each. Some surveyors preferred to use chains with only fifty links. These shorter chains did not tangle as easily as the longer ones. The chain could be wound up and carried over the shoulder.

A compass is the simplest tool for finding directions. It has a round face, similar to a clock's. A compass is marked with **cardinal directions**: north, south, east, and west. The space between each direction is marked as well. A surveyor could find 360 different directions using the **degrees** of the compass circle. This instrument was usually set inside a brass or wooden box.

Make a Shadow Compass

Life in the colonial wilderness could be rough. Surveying teams sometimes lost horses down slippery hillsides, and their supply bags were swept away in raging rivers. The surveyor would not be able to replace his Gunter's chain or **zenith sector** until he got back to civilization. But he could throw together a simple compass anywhere.

This handmade compass took most of a day to make, but it would point due north. That could save the survey team from becoming hopelessly lost. You can make a similar compass and use it to identify the cardinal directions from your garden or school yard.

You Will Need

- a small ball of clay
- a short wooden dowel, approximately 12 inches in length
- a large piece of construction paper (18 x 24 inches is best)
- four paperweights or small rocks
- a permanent marker
- a ruler
- a pencil
- a protractor (optional)
- a sunny day, preferably with little wind
- a flat, open location outside that will be free of shadows all day

(continued)

Instructions

1. Start about 9:00 a.m.

2. Place the ball of clay on a smooth surface. Push it down a bit so that it will not roll.

3. Insert the wooden dowel into the clay. It should go in far enough to stand up straight on its own.

4. Step back and look for the dowel's shadow.

5. If there is no shadow, try again at 10:00 a.m.

6. Lay the paper on the ground. The middle of its long side should touch the clay ball. The dowel's shadow will now fall on the paper and point toward its left edge.

7. Place a weight on each corner of the paper to keep it from blowing away.

8. Use the permanent marker to make a dot at the end of the dowel's shadow.

9. Repeat step 8 every half hour until 3:00 p.m.

10. The paper should now show a semi-circle of eleven to thirteen dots. Carefully draw a line connecting these dots. (Use a protractor if you know how, as this will make a smooth curve

between the dots. The needle of the compass should be placed next to the clay.)

11. Take the ruler and line it up with the center of the clay ball. Now move it slowly along your curved line. Measure the distance between the clay and every dot on your line.

12. Which distance is the shortest? This point on the line represents due north. The clay ball is in the south. Draw a line connecting the two points.

Draw a second line that is perpendicular to your north-south line. (It should cross the first line perfectly, like a plus sign.) This line points east and west. If north is at the top, west is to the left. You now have a compass that tells all the cardinal directions for your current location.

Small, local surveys could be completed using these basic instruments. To conduct large-scale surveys, the apprentice needed to learn the use of sophisticated equipment for calculating latitude and longitude. Latitude indicates how far north or south a place lies from the equator. Longitude measures the position east or west of the Prime Meridian. This imaginary line runs north to south around the globe, passing through Greenwich, England.

Latitude and longitude can be determined by measuring the changing positions of stars over a short period of time. But Earth's rotation and shape make the same stars appear to move differently, depending on the place from which they are observed. The surveyor had to obtain this data each time for every location he visited. He could choose from three instruments, all of which bore telescopes. The **theodolite** and **sextant** were designed to measure a star's angle above the horizon. The zenith sector told him its position compared to the highest point in the sky, or zenith. If he also knew the time, his instrument's reading could be compared to tables listing latitudes and longitudes for the entire world.

Surveyor's Math

The measurement of a property's boundary, or perimeter, was made in chains. However, the government was not interested in perimeters. It wanted to know the area of each piece of land. Area was commonly measured in acres. The acre had been chosen because it described the amount of land one man could work in a day using an ox to pull his plow. One acre represented 43,560 square feet.

The surveyor could use simple arithmetic to calculate the area of any property with a roughly square or rectangular shape. He followed the following steps:

1. Measure the length and width of the land in chains.

2. Convert the measurements from chains to feet. (One chain equals 66 feet.) Multiply the results. This gives the area in square feet.

3. Divide the area (in square feet) by 43,560 to obtain the area in acres.

A common instrument used by colonial surveyors was the theodolite. It measures vertical and horizontal angles.

Higher mathematics was necessary to calculate the area of oddly shaped properties and to measure the height of hills. Even a clever boy had to work hard to learn these difficult skills. It was worth the effort if he wanted to become a master surveyor.

With knowledge under his belt, the apprentice might be invited along on a real survey. He followed his master to observe the use of instruments. He learned to take detailed notes about the property and practiced his calculations. All of these skills would be necessary if he wanted to be hired as a surveyor by the colonial government.

The apprentice was released from his indenture after four to seven years. The next step was to obtain a **license**. He could not conduct surveys for the king and government without this piece of paper. In Virginia, the College of William and Mary gave out all surveying licenses. The young surveyor studied long and hard to take the college's surveying test. A license was his key to the future. A master surveyor might earn more money in a year than a lawyer.

THREE

Dividing the Land

A colonial farmer's main concern was the quality of his land: its access to water, trees, and good soil. He wasted no time selecting a good piece of property as soon as the government told him he was eligible. But most colonial men were not educated in math or measuring, so they often marked out properties of the wrong size. Feuds broke out when colonists disagreed over property lines. In 1688 English surveyor John Love explained the need for professional surveys. He wrote, "For how could men set down to plant, without knowing some distinction and bounds of their land?"

Different Plans

Each colonial government used different methods to survey and divide land. In Virginia and to the south, the system of headright allowed men to pick parcels of land. They chose the best farmland

and stretches of forest that offered woodland for cutting timber. Large areas of swampland and mountainous regions were never surveyed because no one wanted to live there. These parcels of land remained under permanent government ownership. William Penn decided that Pennsylvania would be surveyed in a tidy grid. All of the parcels were shaped like rectangles and laid out side by side. This kept Quaker neighbors close together.

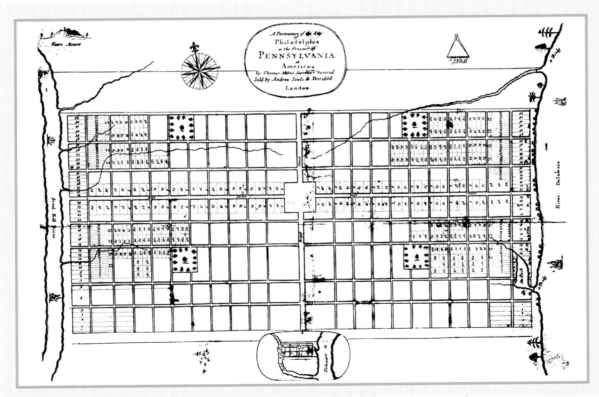

The city of Philadelphia, Pennsylvania, was mapped out in a grid system in 1683.

Puritans in Plymouth, Massachusetts, and in other parts of New England originally hoped to share their property. After arriving in 1620 they built small villages, each with a church at the center and houses located close by. Farmland was situated around the edge of the village. Everyone was supposed to work together, raising food to share. But it soon became clear that this would not work. Like other colonists, Puritans wanted to feel that they owned their land. Their leaders were forced to call in surveyors to split up the farmland.

The size of each man's property was based in part on the number of people in his family. A few additional acres were awarded to men who worked especially hard for the benefit of the community. Puritans valued this kind of service. But they also respected rank. Men who had been wealthy or powerful before moving to the colonies were given a special place in Puritan society and granted additional land.

A Visit to the Surveyor

After choosing his land, a colonist needed to have it surveyed quickly or risk losing the property to someone else, so he rode to the nearest surveyor's office. There was often only one surveyor in each county. It might take the man a day or two of hard travel by horse to reach the surveyor's office. The surveyor wrote down the man's name in his logbook and took notes about the location of the land. The colonist paid a fee, and the surveyor sent a note to the governor asking permission to do a survey. The answer might not come back for days or weeks. Meanwhile the colonist went home to wait.

Once the request had been approved, the surveyor rode out to the property. He often walked the area chosen by the colonist before beginning the survey. This prepared him for challenges and allowed him to make a rough estimate of the property boundaries in advance. Surveyors often went around hills, swamps, and other obstacles. This produced oddly shaped property boundaries, but enclosed the best possible farming land.

If the site was approved, the surveyor was ready to begin a formal measurement of the perimeter. The first step was always to determine a direction in which to lay the chain. The surveyor often mounted his compass atop a tall, wooden rod called a Jacob's staff or held it flat on his hand. Its magnetic needle swung around until the arrow pointed north. The compass had a movable pointer, or sight, that could be slid around the compass wheel. This is called a **sighting**.

One end of the chain was **staked** into the ground at the location of this first sighting. A long, iron pin was pushed through the

Pointing the Way

The compass seems like a straightforward instrument: hold it flat and it points north. True north is located at the earth's North Pole. But compasses rarely point to this location. This is because the earth has a magnetic field. The magnetism pulls a compass arrow away from true north. Surveyors long ago learned to correct for this using a calculation called declination.

The surveyor used two steps to find declination. First, he stayed up at night to find the North Star. This star is directly over the North Pole at a certain time, providing evidence of true north. This location was marked using the compass's movable dial, or clip. While facing true north, the surveyor observed the position of the compass dial. Its black arrow pointed to magnetic north.

Declination is the angle between true north and magnetic north. The surveyor counted the number of degrees between the two points as marked around the edge of the compass. Once declination was determined, the surveyor could adjust his compass to find true north at any location during the survey.

first link and into the ground. The surveyor's assistant, called the **chainman**, walked forward along the sighting line. He slowly unwound the long Gunter's chain as he went. The chainman's most important task was to keep the chain tight and straight so the measurement would be accurate. Sometimes an apprentice was allowed to help in this work. When the chain ran out, the chainman set a stake to mark the spot. Then he walked back and wound up the chain from its beginning. He set the chain at the second stake he'd pushed into the ground, and the process began again. As the team moved along the line, the surveyor stopped now and then to check the sighting on his compass.

The surveyor took a little extra time whenever he reached a corner of the property. He made a deep, clear cut on a tree or other natural object. Called benchmarks, these cuts were intended to show the location of property boundaries. They kept farmers from accidentally planting or hunting on each other's property and helped new colonists see which land was already occupied. In Pennsylvania, farmers were required to refresh their benchmarks every four years for the "preservation of friendship among neighbors."

During these stops the surveyor also wrote down data in his field notebook. How many chains had been measured on that edge of the property? What natural features were present? If there were

A team of surveyors consult their notes and set a line.

hills, the surveyor took time to find their elevation. He set up the
theodolite on a level surface. (This was the same instrument used
to determine latitude and longitude.) A metal bar attached the
theodolite's telescope to a compass below. This compass resembled
the protractors used in school mathematics, with a half-moon
shape and marks to indicate degrees. When the telescope was level,
the bar rested in the middle of the compass. The bar slid forward
along the compass as the surveyor tipped the telescope to sight the
top of the hill. The farther the bar moved from center, the higher
the hill. The surveyor's success depended on accuracy, so he kept
careful track of each detail.

All of this information was used to prepare a map called a **plat**. The surveyor drew every plat by hand, but these were no simple sketches. Ink and watercolor paints showed the boundaries of the property and all of its important features. The surveyor drew the hills he had found, making each one larger or smaller to show its elevation. He carefully outlined the paths of streams and added the locations of lakes or wetlands. Trees were drawn to show different types of forests. If there were signs of minerals in the soil, the surveyor indicated this as well.

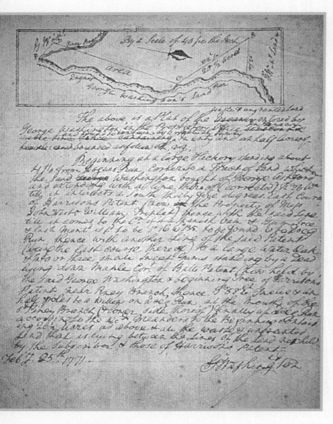

On February 25, 1771, George Washington created this plat of a Virginia property he surveyed.

The completed plat and notes were submitted to the governor's office. The governor had to approve them and put his seal on a **land patent**. This document showed that ownership of the land had been transferred from the king (or William Penn, in Pennsylvania) to a colonist. One copy of the land patent went on file in the surveyor's office. Another copy was delivered to the colonist. With a patent in hand, the man was officially a landowner.

This Land Is My Land

After a colonist's land had been surveyed, he could begin to put up a fence. This served two purposes. The fence was a symbol of his ownership. It stopped other colonists from claiming the land, which would cause an argument. The fence also kept livestock away from his crops.

Some colonists preferred split rail fences. Farmers might sink straight wooden posts into the ground at intervals and connect long rails between them. Simpler split rail fences were made by placing two rails on the ground with their ends overlapping in a V shape. A stack of four or five rails was built atop this base. The fence continued in a zigzag pattern along the border of the property. In later years colonists began to use up their supplies of wood. They had to build stone fences instead. Stone fences were common in the northern colonies. Whenever the farmer's plow struck a stone, he moved it into a pile. The first stones for his wall were placed in a shallow trench, which he dug along the property line. He carefully fitted stones together, filling in the gaps with pebbles. Large, flat stones formed the top layer to keep the wall dry. Such strong walls might last hundreds of years.

FOUR

Laying the Boundaries

Most surveyors worked close to home. They measured headrights and helped divide up property between heirs after a death. They laid out towns and settled arguments about property lines between neighbors. But a few of the most highly skilled surveyors were hired to conduct boundary surveys. Boundary surveys were used to determine the official borders between colonies.

A small-scale surveyor worked with a few assistants. On average, he surveyed less than six miles per day. This was rarely easy work, and boundary surveys made typical surveys look simple. The challenges are well represented by the 1728 survey of the border between Virginia and North Carolina. That spring lead surveyors William Byrd II and William Mayo set off into the wilderness. More than twenty men were in their party: chainmen, boundary markers, woodsmen to cut trees, cooks, horse handlers, and more. The first Gunter's chain was set alongside Chesapeake Bay, beside the Atlantic Ocean. From that point the surveyors moved in a straight line to the west. The line cut through thick forests and swamplands. William Byrd described the conditions, saying, "The Ground, if I may properly call it so, was so Spungy, that the Prints of our Feet were instantly fill'd with Water." The team was gone for months, finally surveying more than 170 miles along this important colonial boundary.

The surveyor was expected to be equally honest and exact however large or small the project. To prove his commitment, he took an oath before beginning each job:

I do solemnly swear that I will truthfully and faithfully discharge and execute the duties as land surveyor to the best of my knowledge and power and I will use equipment that measures justly and exactly.

Into the Wilderness

The boundary surveyor depended on his large team of assistants. Some workers walked ahead of the chainmen, hanging flags to show where the chain should be laid. If the woods were very thick, the surveyor used woodsmen to cut down trees. This provided a clear view so he could make sure that the line was still being laid in the right direction.

It was also common to build permanent markers along colonial boundary lines. These benchmarks were often made from large piles of stones. When the boundary between Pennsylvania and Maryland was surveyed in 1763, every benchmark was specially marked. The letter *M* was painted on the south side, showing that

The surveyor relied on his assistants when setting property boundaries.

Maryland lay in that direction. The north side of each stone read *P* for Pennsylvania. Certain benchmarks along the line included the elaborate coat of arms of the Penn family.

To speed up the work, the surveyor might use the ride-and-tie system. At the beginning of the day, team members were assigned to groups. Half of each group began to survey the line on foot. The other half rode ahead on horseback. After a certain distance they tied up the horses and began to walk ahead, surveying the line as they went. When the first men reached the horses, they untied them and rode past their teammates. This leapfrogging system continued throughout the day. It kept the men from becoming too weary and allowed them to survey more ground.

The surveyor and his team carried all of their belongings in backpacks and on horses. At the end of the day, the team set up tents and made a campfire. They always carried dried meat and fruit, but it helped to find supplies along the way. The men hunted, fished, and gathered what they could from the land. Bad weather didn't stop the survey. If it rained, the surveyor and his team huddled in their tents and drew maps while they waited for the weather to clear.

When the job was finished, the surveyor could count on a good income. Pennsylvania surveyors charged for every mile surveyed, adding a fee for preparing the plat. In Virginia tobacco was often

Surveying teams ended their long days in the countryside around a campfire.

used as currency. Surveyors charged 40 pounds of tobacco for each 100 acres of land surveyed. They kept 5 percent of this, turning the remainder over to the government. This valuable crop could be sold for cash. Surveyors often took land in payment for their services, as well. Owning land gave the surveyor power in his community.

Cities and Roads

As the colonial population grew, demand increased for towns and roads. The surveyor knew the land better than anyone. He showed government officials where good sources of water and wood could be found, and laid out the plans for streets and buildings. The next step was to engineer roads connecting these growing villages and cities. Early colonial roads were often nothing more than rambling, rough horse and wagon tracks. The surveyor found ways to straighten and shorten the roads, making it quicker to move throughout the colonies.

William Penn wanted his colony to have a "great towne." Covering 10,000 acres, Philadelphia would be the largest colonial city yet built. In 1682 Penn sat down with a surveyor named Thomas Holme. Together they drew up plans for a city with parallel streets that led toward a central square and the Delaware River. Green fields bordered the entire city. Penn hoped that Philadelphia would be a healthy and happy place for its residents. It became a model for later cities that grew up in the colonies.

Philadelphia, Pennsylvania, was planned with parallel streets, a central square, and was surrounded with green fields.

A Man in His Community

The surveyor was often among the most educated men in his community. Also, he was highly paid for his work, which should have made him wealthy. However, surveying work was uncertain. Many requests for land patents might be submitted at once, then none for months afterward. The surveyor typically needed a second occupation to support his family. He might raise crops on his farm, or buy and sell land as a **speculator**. Some surveyors were merchants, innkeepers, or even lawyers. Others made the instruments used in surveying or were professional mapmakers.

Surveyors were also dedicated members of their communities. They were involved in the church and other community organizations. Many ran for public offices, becoming local sheriffs or taking positions in colonial government. Pennsylvania surveyor John Morton provides a remarkable example. He was elected a justice of the peace in 1756. Like a judge, he was responsible for trying minor crimes and lawsuits in his community. Morton was later appointed a Pennsylvania supreme court judge and went on to sign the Declaration of Independence.

The Call for More Land

The demand for colonial land became tremendous in the early 1700s. People arrived and did not worry about whether the

Whose America Is This?

When colonists arrived in America, they did not find an empty land. There were millions of American-Indian peoples living on the continent. Some tribes built houses and kept farms. Others traveled from place to place, following food sources as they became available through the seasons. Each tribe might protect its territory from neighbors, but there were no fences. American Indians did not think it was necessary to divide up the earth.

Englishmen believed that man was meant to own and control the land. The only way to prove ownership was to put up fences. This was called enclosure. There were a few colonial leaders who respected the American Indians. They said that England should have to buy property from tribes. Other colonists laughed at this idea. They said that the American colonies belonged to them and they could use the land freely.

land belonged to someone else. They settled anywhere there was open space. Rumor said that America's best farmlands lay in the valleys west of the Appalachian Mountains. This land was already home to many American-Indian tribes and had been settled by French colonists.

English troops and colonists fought France for control of this land. American-Indian tribes either took sides or tried to stay out of the way. The French eventually signed a treaty giving up all their land east of the Mississippi River to England. But England's King George III shocked the colonists by refusing to allow surveys or settlement of the newly acquired territory. He wrote that "great Frauds and Abuses have been committed in the purchasing [of] Lands of the Indians." All settlers were required to remain east of the Appalachian Mountains, in the original colonies.

Some colonists began to resist the English government's control. They would soon start a revolution to gain independence. The surveyor would play a crucial role as millions of Americans set off to explore and settle the United States of America.

Glossary

acre	a unit for measuring the area of land, equal to 43,560 square feet
apprentice	a person who trains to learn a new skill or job by working with an expert
cardinal directions	north, south, east, and west
chainman	a surveyor's assistant
compass	a scientific instrument used to find directions
degrees	the 360 units of a circle, used to tell small differences in direction on a compass
elevation	the height of land above sea level
headright	land given to colonists who paid for passage from England
indenture	a contract requiring a person to serve an employer for some period of years as a worker or apprentice
land patent	a document showing ownership of land
license	a document that gives permission to do work
plat	a map showing the boundaries of property plus the features of the landscape
sextant	an instrument used to measure the angle of stars above the hoizon
shareholder	a person who gives money to support a company
sighting	the direction indicated by a compass being used to show the line of a survey chain
speculator	a person who buys land and resells it for a profit
stake	a metal rod pushed into the ground to hold something in place
theodolite	similar to a sextant, but designed to measure horizontal and vertical angles
zenith sector	an instrument used to measure the position of stars compared to the highest point in the night sky

Find Out More

BOOKS

Kalkhoven, Laurie. *George Washington: An American Life.* New York: Sterling Publishing, 2007.

Kalman, Bobbie. *A Visual Dictionary of a Colonial Community.* New York: Crabtree Publishing Company, 2008.

Mara, Wil. *The Farmer.* New York: Marshall Cavendish Benchmark, 2010.

Roberts, Russell. *Life in Colonial America.* Hockessin, DE: Mitchell Lane Publishers, 2007.

WEBSITES

Colonial Williamsburg Kids Zone

www.history.org/kids/

Tour the colonial capital of Virginia and meet some of its important residents. There are games, activities, and many resources about colonial life and history.

Rare Map Collection—Colonial America

www.libs.uga.edu/darchive/hargrett/maps/colamer.html

Interested in old maps? This site from the University of Georgia contains dozens of images of original maps dating back to the colonial period.

Washington's Boyhood

www.kenmore.org/ferryfarm/boyhood.html

Learn more about George Washington's early life.

Index

About the Author

Christine Petersen has written more than three dozen books and several magazine articles for a variety of audiences, from emerging readers to adults. Her subjects include science, nature, and social studies. When she's not writing, Petersen and her young son enjoy exploring the natural areas near their home in Minneapolis, Minnesota. Petersen is a member of the Society of Children's Book Writers and Illustrators.